"You don't become what you want, you become what you believe." - Oprah Winfrey

A "Mary E's Read" Imprint

© O.T.M PUBLISHING 2022

TREE
LIKE
ME
Written by: Kiara Johnson

There are trees like me?

Yes there are trees like you!

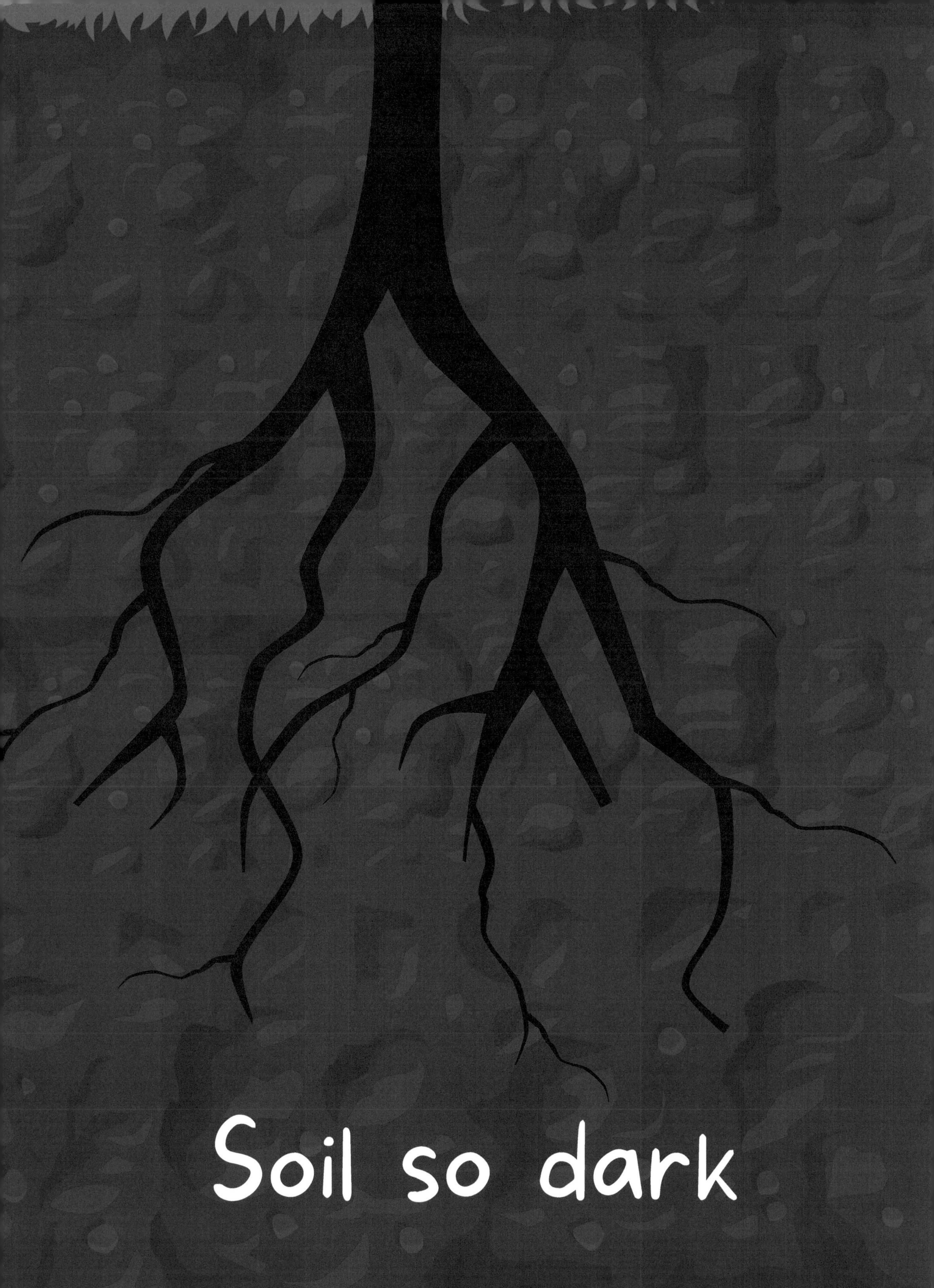
Soil so dark

Surrounding all of
these deep roots!

We plant all of
these trees

We eat all of their fruits

We breathe
trees in

THEN

O₂
O₂
O₂
O₂
O₂
O₂
O₂
O₂
O₂
POOF!

I want to be a tree.

Oh do you now?

Do you want to
be a big tree?

One that stretches
to the clouds?

I want to be big enough
Spread love!
Just believe!
Never give up!

So that everyone can see me!

But then you would block the
Sun

How would we get the
light that we need?

It's okay
to be a tree,

Be the tree that
everyone needs.

Shade people
on hot days.

Give the squirrels something to eat.

Let the children come and play.

Be a home for
the birds to sing.

Remain strong
through it all.

No matter
what the day
may bring.

When the storm
is over,

You will come
out clean!

So I will be a
tree like you?

And you will
be a tree like
me!